THIS BOOK BELONGS TO:

_____

Published by Citrine A

Words Of Encouragement

Wash your hands!

This will be a challenge for a lot of you, but YOU CAN DO IT!

One day all your thumbs up will be colored in and you will feel clean and proud, knowing that washing hands wasn't as hard as you first thought it to be!

Let's get going!

Monday

Color in all the thumbs up that apply
ON THE NEXT PAGE!

 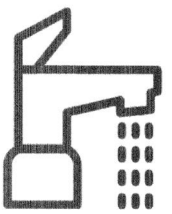

I WASHED MY HANDS...

MONDAY

Every time after going to 👍
the bathroom!

Before Breakfast 👍

After shaking hands 👍

Before lunch 👍

After going to the store or 👍
socializing

After work/meetings 👍

Before dinner 👍

Before bed 👍

Super job washing hands! Color these cool water drops in diffrent shades of BLUE!

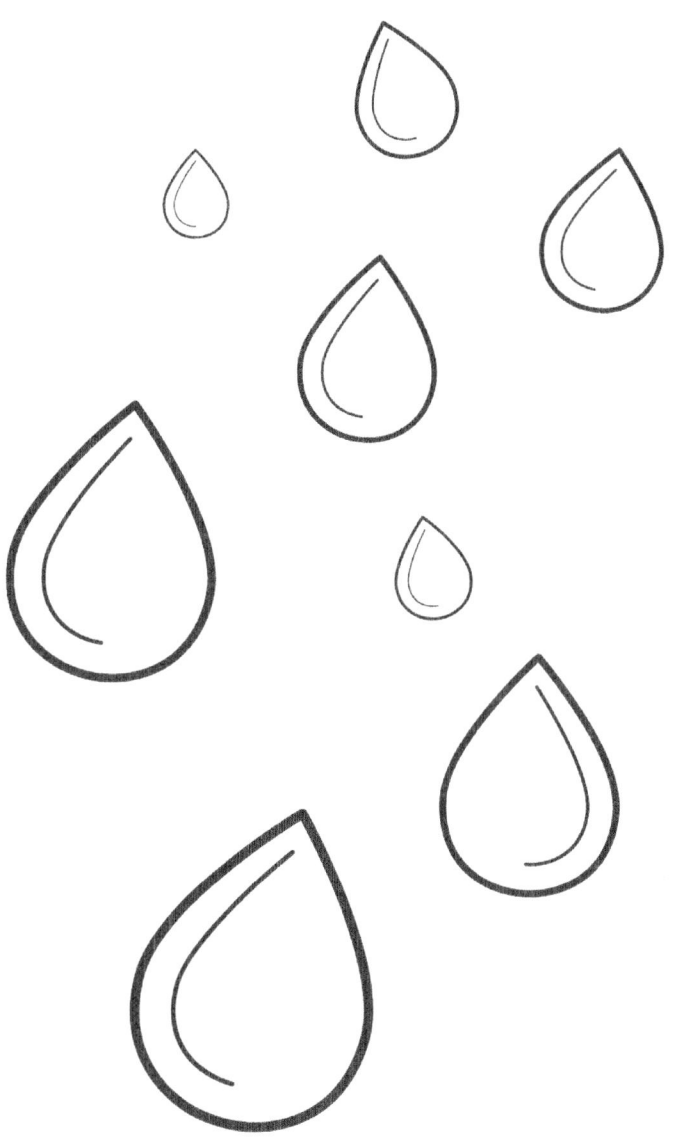

Tuesday

Color in all the thumbs up that apply
ON THE NEXT PAGE!

I WASHED MY HANDS...

TUESDAY

Every time after going to 👍
the bathroom!

Before Breakfast 👍

After shaking hands 👍

Before lunch 👍

After going to the store or 👍
socializing

After work/meetings 👍

Before dinner 👍

Before bed 👍

Super job washing hands! Color these cool water drops in diffrent shades of PINK/PURPLE!

Wednesday

Color in all the thumbs up that apply
ON THE NEXT PAGE!

I WASHED MY HANDS...

WEDNESDAY

Every time after going to 👍
the bathroom!

Before Breakfast 👍

After shaking hands 👍

Before lunch 👍

After going to the store or 👍
socializing

After work/meetings 👍

Before dinner 👍

Before bed 👍

Super job washing hands! Color these cool water drops in diffrent shades of GREEN!

Thursday

Color in all the thumbs up that apply
ON THE NEXT PAGE!

I WASHED MY HANDS...

THURSDAY

Every time after going to 👍
the bathroom!

Before Breakfast 👍

After shaking hands 👍

Before lunch 👍

After going to the store or 👍
socializing

After work/meetings 👍

Before dinner 👍

Before bed 👍

Super job washing hands! Color these cool water drops in diffrent shades of YELLOW!

Friday

Color in all the thumbs up that apply
ON THE NEXT PAGE!

I WASHED MY HANDS...

FRIDAY

Every time after going to 👍
the bathroom!

Before Breakfast 👍

After shaking hands 👍

Before lunch 👍

After going to the store or 👍
socializing

After work/meetings 👍

Before dinner 👍

Before bed 👍

Super job washing hands! Color these cool water drops in diffrent shades of RED/ORANGE!

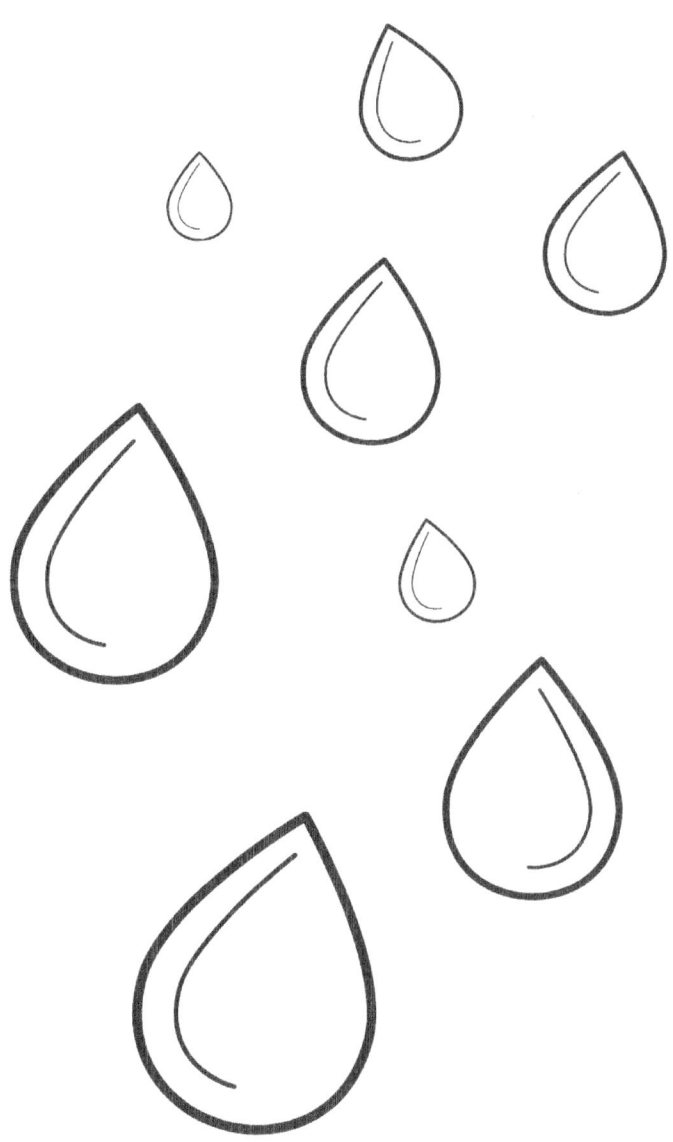

Saturday

Color in all the thumbs up that apply ON THE NEXT PAGE!

I WASHED MY HANDS...

SATURDAY

Every time after going to 👍
the bathroom!

Before Breakfast 👍

After shaking hands 👍

Before lunch 👍

After going to the store or 👍
socializing

After work/meetings 👍

Before dinner 👍

Before bed 👍

Super job washing hands! Color these cool water drops in RAINBOW COLORS !

Sunday

Color in all the thumbs up that apply
ON THE NEXT PAGE!

I WASHED MY HANDS...

SUNDAY

Every time after going to 👍
the bathroom!

Before Breakfast 👍

After shaking hands 👍

Before lunch 👍

After going to the store or 👍
socializing

After work/meetings 👍

Before dinner 👍

Before bed 👍

SUNDAY, FUN DAY! DRAW WHATEVER YOU WANT!

You DESERVE IT!

My progress:

My thumbs up are partially colored in at this point ☐

My thumbs up are all colored in at this point ☐

Every day is different. Sometimes they are all colored in, some days they are partially colored in ☐

The hardest part of this exercise for me is:

The week is done, let's start a new week!

Monday

Color in all the thumbs up that apply
ON THE NEXT PAGE!

I WASHED MY HANDS...

MONDAY

Every time after going to 👍
the bathroom!

Before Breakfast 👍

After shaking hands 👍

Before lunch 👍

After going to the store or 👍
socializing

After work/meetings 👍

Before dinner 👍

Before bed 👍

Super job washing hands! Color these cool water drops in diffrent shades of BLUE!

Tuesday

Color in all the thumbs up that apply
ON THE NEXT PAGE!

I WASHED MY HANDS...

TUESDAY

Every time after going to 👍
the bathroom!

Before Breakfast 👍

After shaking hands 👍

Before lunch 👍

After going to the store or 👍
socializing

After work/meetings 👍

Before dinner 👍

Before bed 👍

Super job washing hands! Color these cool water drops in diffrent shades of PINK/PURPLE!

Wednesday

Color in all the thumbs up that apply
ON THE NEXT PAGE!

I WASHED MY HANDS...

WEDNESDAY

Every time after going to the bathroom! 👍

Before Breakfast 👍

After shaking hands 👍

Before lunch 👍

After going to the store or socializing 👍

After work/meetings 👍

Before dinner 👍

Before bed 👍

Super job washing hands! Color these cool water drops in diffrent shades of GREEN!

Thursday

Color in all the thumbs up that apply
ON THE NEXT PAGE!

I WASHED MY HANDS...

THURSDAY

Every time after going to 👍
the bathroom!

Before Breakfast 👍

After shaking hands 👍

Before lunch 👍

After going to the store or 👍
socializing

After work/meetings 👍

Before dinner 👍

Before bed 👍

Super job washing hands! Color these cool water drops in diffrent shades of YELLOW!

Friday

Color in all the thumbs up that apply
ON THE NEXT PAGE!

I WASHED MY HANDS...

FRIDAY

Every time after going to 👍
the bathroom!

Before Breakfast 👍

After shaking hands 👍

Before lunch 👍

After going to the store or 👍
socializing

After work/meetings 👍

Before dinner 👍

Before bed  👍

Super job washing hands! Color these cool water drops in diffrent shades of RED/ORANGE!

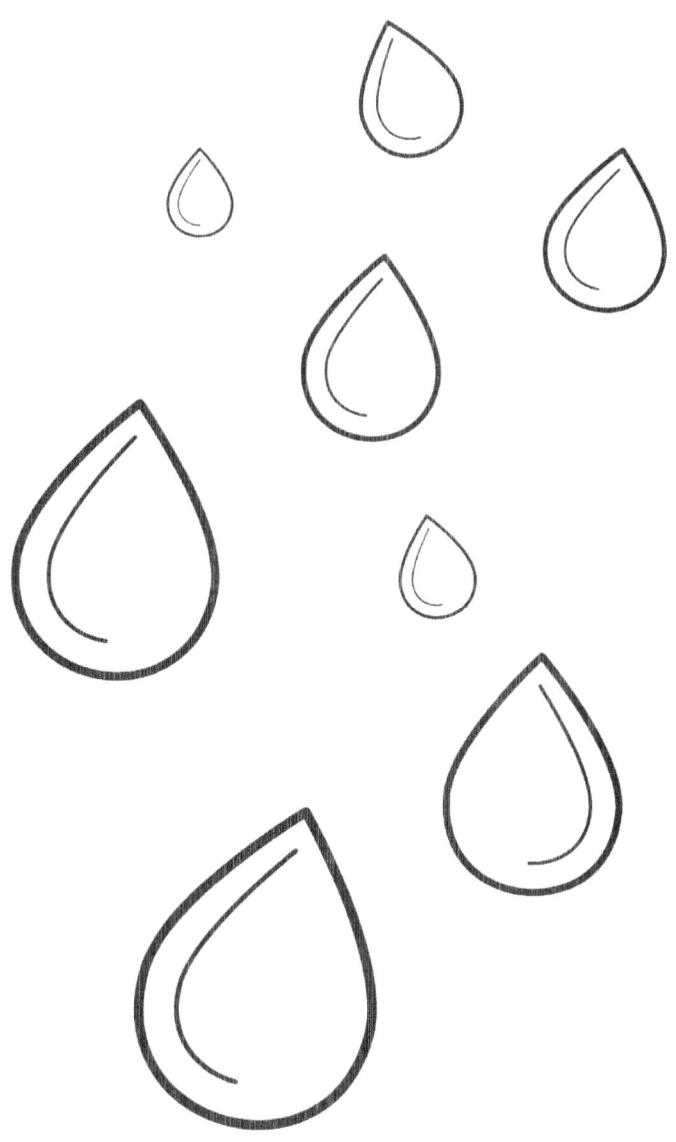

Saturday

Color in all the thumbs up that apply
ON THE NEXT PAGE!

I WASHED MY HANDS...

SATURDAY

Every time after going to 👍
the bathroom!

Before Breakfast 👍

After shaking hands 👍

Before lunch 👍

After going to the store or 👍
socializing

After work/meetings 👍

Before dinner 👍

Before bed 👍

Super job washing hands! Color these cool water drops in RAINBOW COLORS !

Sunday

Color in all the thumbs up that apply
ON THE NEXT PAGE!

I WASHED MY HANDS...

SUNDAY

Every time after going to the bathroom! 👍

Before Breakfast 👍

After shaking hands 👍

Before lunch 👍

After going to the store or socializing 👍

After work/meetings 👍

Before dinner 👍

Before bed 👍

SUNDAY, FUN DAY! DRAW WHATEVER YOU WANT!

You DESERVE IT!

My progress:

My thumbs up are partially colored in at this point ☐

My thumbs up are all colored in at this point ☐

Every day is different. Sometimes they are all colored in, some days they are partially colored in ☐

The hardest part of this exercise for me is:

THE WEEK IS DONE, LET'S START A NEW WEEK!

Color in all the thumbs up that apply
ON THE NEXT PAGE!

I WASHED MY HANDS...

MONDAY

Every time after going to 👍
the bathroom!

Before Breakfast 👍

After shaking hands 👍

Before lunch 👍

After going to the store or 👍
socializing

After work/meetings 👍

Before dinner 👍

Before bed 👍

Super job washing hands! Color these cool water drops in diffrent shades of BLUE!

Tuesday

Color in all the thumbs up that apply
ON THE NEXT PAGE!

I WASHED MY HANDS...

TUESDAY

Every time after going to 👍
the bathroom!

Before Breakfast 👍

After shaking hands 👍

Before lunch 👍

After going to the store or 👍
socializing

After work/meetings 👍

Before dinner 👍

Before bed 👍

Super job washing hands! Color these cool water drops in diffrent shades of PINK/PURPLE!

Wednesday

Color in all the thumbs up that apply
ON THE NEXT PAGE!

I WASHED MY HANDS...

WEDNESDAY

Every time after going to 👍
the bathroom!

Before Breakfast 👍

After shaking hands 👍

Before lunch 👍

After going to the store or 👍
socializing

After work/meetings 👍

Before dinner 👍

Before bed 👍

Super job washing hands! Color these cool water drops in diffrent shades of GREEN!

Thursday

Color in all the thumbs up that apply
ON THE NEXT PAGE!

I WASHED MY HANDS...

THURSDAY

Every time after going to 👍
the bathroom!

Before Breakfast 👍

After shaking hands 👍

Before lunch 👍

After going to the store or 👍
socializing

After work/meetings 👍

Before dinner 👍

Before bed 👍

Super job washing hands! Color these cool water drops in diffrent shades of YELLOW!

Friday

Color in all the thumbs up that apply
ON THE NEXT PAGE!

I WASHED MY HANDS...

FRIDAY

Every time after going to 👍
the bathroom!

Before Breakfast 👍

After shaking hands 👍

Before lunch 👍

After going to the store or 👍
socializing

After work/meetings 👍

Before dinner 👍

Before bed 👍

Super job washing hands! Color these cool water drops in diffrent shades of RED/ORANGE!

Saturday

Color in all the thumbs up that apply
ON THE NEXT PAGE!

I WASHED MY HANDS...

SATURDAY

Every time after going to 👍
the bathroom!

Before Breakfast 👍

After shaking hands 👍

Before lunch 👍

After going to the store or 👍
socializing

After work/meetings 👍

Before dinner 👍

Before bed 👍

Super job washing hands! Color these cool water drops in RAINBOW COLORS !

Sunday

Color in all the thumbs up that apply
ON THE NEXT PAGE!

I WASHED MY HANDS...

SUNDAY

Every time after going to 👍
the bathroom!

Before Breakfast 👍

After shaking hands 👍

Before lunch 👍

After going to the store or 👍
socializing

After work/meetings 👍

Before dinner 👍

Before bed 👍

SUNDAY, FUN DAY! DRAW WHATEVER YOU WANT!

YOU DESERVE IT!

My PROGRESS:

My thumbs up are partially
colored in at this point

My thumbs up are all colored in at
this point

Every day is different. Sometimes
they are all colored in, some days
they are partially colored in

The hardest part of this
exercise for me is:

THE WEEK IS DONE,
LET'S START a
new week!

Monday

Color in all the thumbs up that apply
ON THE NEXT PAGE!

I WASHED MY HANDS...

MONDAY

Every time after going to the bathroom! 👍

Before Breakfast 👍

After shaking hands 👍

Before lunch 👍

After going to the store or socializing 👍

After work/meetings 👍

Before dinner 👍

Before bed 👍

Super job washing hands! Color these cool water drops in diffrent shades of BLUE!

Tuesday

Color in all the thumbs up that apply
ON THE NEXT PAGE!

I WASHED MY HANDS...

TUESDAY

Every time after going to 👍
the bathroom!

Before Breakfast 👍

After shaking hands 👍

Before lunch 👍

After going to the store or 👍
socializing

After work/meetings 👍

Before dinner 👍

Before bed 👍

Super job washing hands! Color
these cool water drops in
diffrent shades of
PINK/PURPLE!

Wednesday

Color in all the thumbs up that apply
ON THE NEXT PAGE!

I WASHED MY HANDS...

WEDNESDAY

Every time after going to 👍
the bathroom!

Before Breakfast 👍

After shaking hands 👍

Before lunch 👍

After going to the store or 👍
socializing

After work/meetings 👍

Before dinner 👍

Before bed 👍

Super job washing hands! Color these cool water drops in diffrent shades of GREEN!

Thursday

Color in all the thumbs up that apply ON THE NEXT PAGE!

I WASHED MY HANDS...

THURSDAY

Every time after going to 👍
the bathroom!

Before Breakfast 👍

After shaking hands 👍

Before lunch 👍

After going to the store or 👍
socializing

After work/meetings 👍

Before dinner 👍

Before bed 👍

Super job washing hands! Color these cool water drops in diffrent shades of YELLOW!

Friday

Color in all the thumbs up that apply
ON THE NEXT PAGE!

I WASHED MY HANDS...

FRIDAY

Every time after going to 👍
the bathroom!

Before Breakfast 👍

After shaking hands 👍

Before lunch 👍

After going to the store or 👍
socializing

After work/meetings 👍

Before dinner 👍

Before bed 👍

Super job washing hands! Color these cool water drops in diffrent shades of RED/ORANGE!

Saturday

Color in all the thumbs up that apply
ON THE NEXT PAGE!

I WASHED MY HANDS...

SATURDAY

Every time after going to 👍
the bathroom!

Before Breakfast 👍

After shaking hands 👍

Before lunch 👍

After going to the store or 👍
socializing

After work/meetings 👍

Before dinner 👍

Before bed 👍

Super job washing hands! Color these cool water drops in RAINBOW COLORS !

Sunday

Color in all the thumbs up that apply
ON THE NEXT PAGE!

I WASHED MY HANDS...

SUNDAY

Every time after going to 👍
the bathroom!

Before Breakfast 👍

After shaking hands 👍

Before lunch 👍

After going to the store or 👍
socializing

After work/meetings 👍

Before dinner 👍

Before bed 👍

SUNDAY, FUN DAY! DRAW WHATEVER YOU WANT!

You DESERVE IT!

My progress:

My thumbs up are partially colored in at this point ☐

My thumbs up are all colored in at this point ☐

Every day is different. Sometimes they are all colored in, some days they are partially colored in ☐

The hardest part of this exercise for me is:

The week is done, let's start a new week!

Monday

Color in all the thumbs up that apply
ON THE NEXT PAGE!

I WASHED MY HANDS...

MONDAY

Every time after going to 👍
the bathroom!

Before Breakfast 👍

After shaking hands 👍

Before lunch 👍

After going to the store or 👍
socializing

After work/meetings 👍

Before dinner 👍

Before bed 👍

Super job washing hands! Color these cool water drops in diffrent shades of BLUE!

Tuesday

Color in all the thumbs up that apply
ON THE NEXT PAGE!

I WASHED MY HANDS...

TUESDAY

Every time after going to 👍
the bathroom!

Before Breakfast 👍

After shaking hands 👍

Before lunch 👍

After going to the store or 👍
socializing

After work/meetings 👍

Before dinner 👍

Before bed 👍

Super job washing hands! Color these cool water drops in diffrent shades of PINK/PURPLE!

Wednesday

Color in all the thumbs up that apply
ON THE NEXT PAGE!

I WASHED MY HANDS...

WEDNESDAY

Every time after going to 👍
the bathroom!

Before Breakfast 👍

After shaking hands 👍

Before lunch 👍

After going to the store or 👍
socializing

After work/meetings 👍

Before dinner 👍

Before bed 👍

Super job washing hands! Color these cool water drops in diffrent shades of GREEN!

Thursday

Color in all the thumbs up that apply
ON THE NEXT PAGE!

I WASHED MY HANDS...

THURSDAY

Every time after going to 👍
the bathroom!

Before Breakfast 👍

After shaking hands 👍

Before lunch 👍

After going to the store or 👍
socializing

After work/meetings 👍

Before dinner 👍

Before bed 👍

Super job washing hands! Color these cool water drops in diffrent shades of YELLOW!

Friday

Color in all the thumbs up that apply
ON THE NEXT PAGE!

I WASHED MY HANDS...

FRIDAY

Every time after going to 👍
the bathroom!

Before Breakfast 👍

After shaking hands 👍

Before lunch 👍

After going to the store or 👍
socializing

After work/meetings 👍

Before dinner 👍

Before bed 👍

Super job washing hands! Color these cool water drops in diffrent shades of RED/ORANGE!

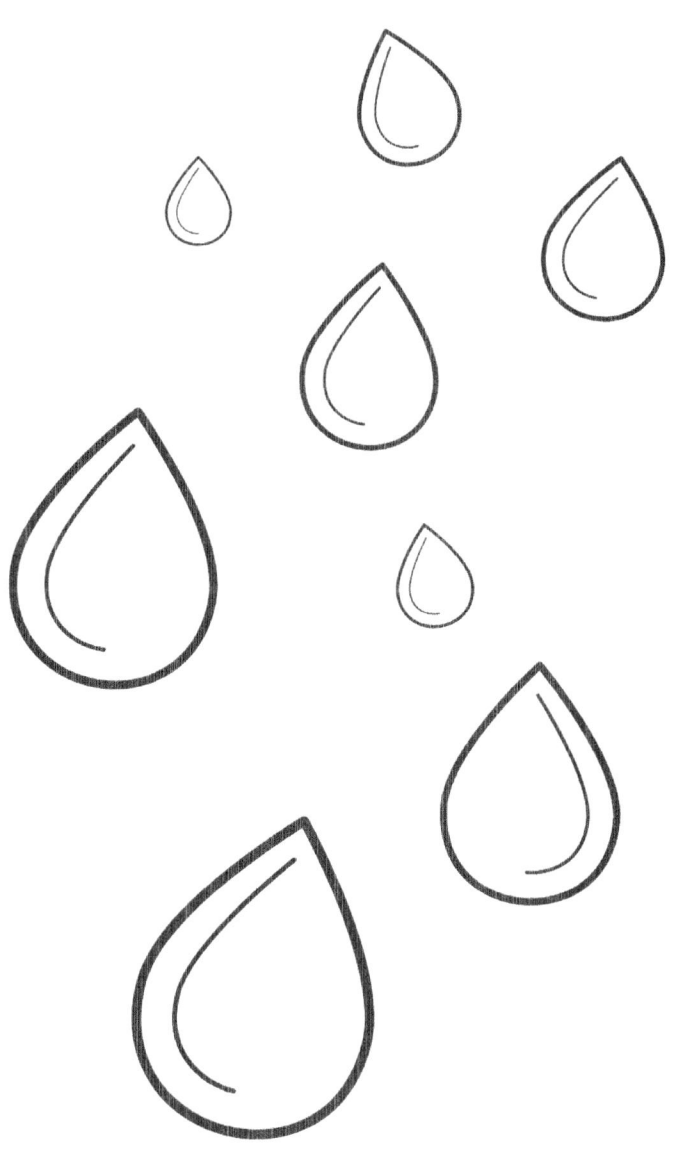

Saturday

Color in all the thumbs up that apply
ON THE NEXT PAGE!

I WASHED MY HANDS...

SATURDAY

Every time after going to 👍
the bathroom!

Before Breakfast 👍

After shaking hands 👍

Before lunch 👍

After going to the store or 👍
socializing

After work/meetings 👍

Before dinner 👍

Before bed 👍

Super job washing hands! Color these cool water drops in RAINBOW COLORS !

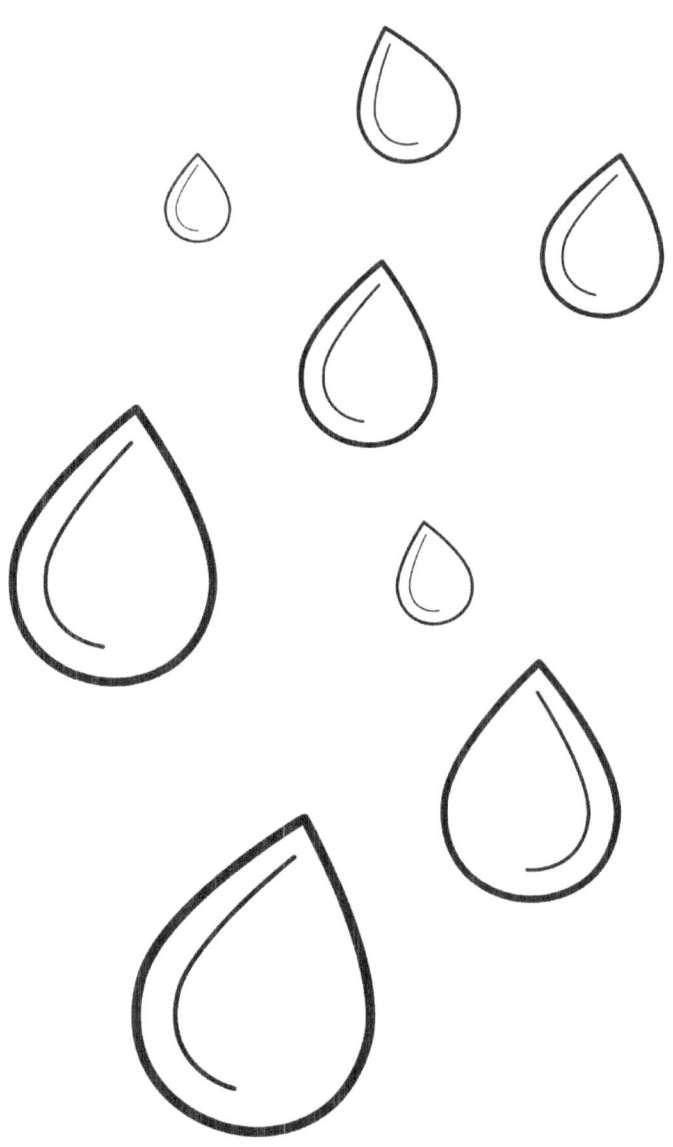

Sunday

Color in all the thumbs up that apply
ON THE NEXT PAGE!

I WASHED MY HANDS...

SUNDAY

Every time after going to 👍
the bathroom!

Before Breakfast 👍

After shaking hands 👍

Before lunch 👍

After going to the store or 👍
socializing

After work/meetings 👍

Before dinner 👍

Before bed 👍

SUNDAY, FUN DAY! DRAW WHATEVER YOU WANT!

You DESERVE IT!

My progress:

My thumbs up are partially colored in at this point ☐

My thumbs up are all colored in at this point ☐

Every day is different. Sometimes they are all colored in, some days they are partially colored in ☐

The hardest part of this exercise for me is:

The week is done, let's start a new week!

Monday

Color in all the thumbs up that apply
ON THE NEXT PAGE!

I WASHED MY HANDS...

MONDAY

Every time after going to 👍 the bathroom!

Before Breakfast 👍

After shaking hands 👍

Before lunch 👍

After going to the store or 👍 socializing

After work/meetings 👍

Before dinner 👍

Before bed 👍

Super job washing hands! Color these cool water drops in diffrent shades of BLUE!

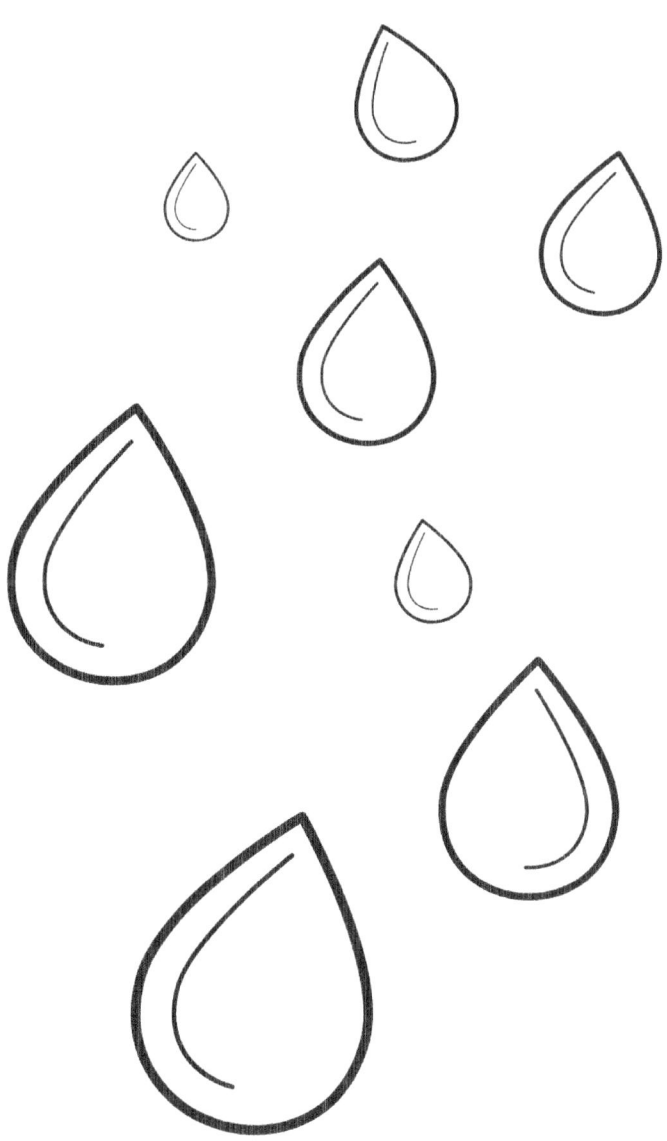

Tuesday

Color in all the thumbs up that apply
ON THE NEXT PAGE!

I WASHED MY HANDS...

TUESDAY

Every time after going to 👍
the bathroom!

Before Breakfast 👍

After shaking hands 👍

Before lunch 👍

After going to the store or 👍
socializing

After work/meetings 👍

Before dinner 👍

Before bed 👍

Super job washing hands! Color these cool water drops in diffrent shades of PINK/PURPLE!

Wednesday

Color in all the thumbs up that apply
ON THE NEXT PAGE!

I WASHED MY HANDS...

WEDNESDAY

Every time after going to 👍
the bathroom!

Before Breakfast 👍

After shaking hands 👍

Before lunch 👍

After going to the store or 👍
socializing

After work/meetings 👍

Before dinner 👍

Before bed 👍

Super job washing hands! Color these cool water drops in diffrent shades of GREEN!

Thursday

Color in all the thumbs up that apply
ON THE NEXT PAGE!

I WASHED MY HANDS...

THURSDAY

Every time after going to 👍
the bathroom!

Before Breakfast 👍

After shaking hands 👍

Before lunch 👍

After going to the store or 👍
socializing

After work/meetings 👍

Before dinner 👍

Before bed 👍

Super job washing hands! Color these cool water drops in diffrent shades of YELLOW!

Friday

Color in all the thumbs up that apply
ON THE NEXT PAGE!

I WASHED MY HANDS...

FRIDAY

Every time after going to 👍
the bathroom!

Before Breakfast 👍

After shaking hands 👍

Before lunch 👍

After going to the store or 👍
socializing

After work/meetings 👍

Before dinner 👍

Before bed 👍

Super job washing hands! Color these cool water drops in diffrent shades of RED/ORANGE!

Saturday

Color in all the thumbs up that apply
ON THE NEXT PAGE!

I WASHED MY HANDS...

SATURDAY

Every time after going to 👍
the bathroom!

Before Breakfast 👍

After shaking hands 👍

Before lunch 👍

After going to the store or 👍
socializing

After work/meetings 👍

Before dinner 👍

Before bed 👍

Super job washing hands! Color these cool water drops in RAINBOW COLORS !

Sunday

Color in all the thumbs up that apply
ON THE NEXT PAGE!

I WASHED MY HANDS...

SUNDAY

Every time after going to 👍
the bathroom!

Before Breakfast 👍

After shaking hands 👍

Before lunch 👍

After going to the store or 👍
socializing

After work/meetings 👍

Before dinner 👍

Before bed 👍

SUNDAY, FUN DAY! DRAW WHATEVER YOU WANT!

You DESERVE IT!

My progress
throughout the weeks:

My thumbs up are still partially colored in ☐

My thumbs up are all colored in at this point ☐

Every day is still different. Some days they are all colored in, some days they are partially colored in ☐

What I learn from this exercise...

YOU DID GREAT! KEEP ON WASHING YOUR HANDS. THUMBS UP!

Printed in Great Britain
by Amazon